Building Confidence for Teens In School and In Life

By Jean Young

EXPERIENCE EVERYTHING
P U B L I S H I N G

Disclaimer

This document is geared towards providing exact and reliable information in regards to the topic and issue covered. The publication is sold with the idea that the publisher is not required to render accounting, officially permitted, or otherwise, qualified services. If advice is necessary, legal or professional, a practiced individual in the profession should be ordered.

- From a Declaration of Principles which was accepted and approved equally by a Committee of the American Bar Association and a Committee of Publishers and Associations:

The information provided herein is stated to be truthful and consistent, in that any liability, in terms of inattention or otherwise, by any usage or abuse of any policies, processes, or directions contained within is the solitary and utter responsibility of the recipient reader. Under no circumstances will any legal responsibility or blame be held against the publisher for any reparation, damages, or monetary loss due to the information herein, either directly or indirectly.

The information herein is offered for informational purposes solely, and is universal as so. The presentation of the information is without contract or any type of guarantee assurance.

The trademarks that are used are without any consent, and the publication of the trademark is without permission or backing by the trademark owner. All trademarks and brands within this book are for clarifying purposes only and are the owned by the owners themselves, not affiliated with this document.

Introduction

Our teenage years is the time of our lives when we go through so many changes. This is the time when start to discover who we really are and it is also when the beliefs we had as kids start to change. Even our body goes through so many changes during our teenage years. At this time of change, it is also important that we remain to be confident in ourselves and the things that we do. Even in our teenage years, we need to understand that we can accomplish whatever it is that we want to accomplish as long as we work for it.

Why is confidence important during the teenage years?

As a general rule in life, confidence is a must. But it is even more important in the teenage years because of the many changes that a teen has to go through. Teenagers move from middle school to high school and then from high school to college. As these changes in the school environment happens, a teen will also need to go through various changes and challenges. Despite the difficulties that could arise, a confident teen will be able to overcome these various changes. Here are some good reasons why confidence is important in a teenager's life:

1. Teenagers will have to tackle many difficult situations and, in order for them to bounce right back from a challenging situation, they need to be resilient and strong. A teen has to be strong mentally in order to convince themself that they have what it takes to overcome these changes and challenges. A teen that does not have enough confidence will also not have a good self-esteem. They consider themself to be weak and unable to overcome such challenges.

2. For any person to make a good decision, it is important for them to have the right confidence and being able to follow through with whatever decision they have made. For a teen, it is really important because teens who do not have enough confidence are likely to fall into the traps of peer pressure. They will not be able to avoid the things and people that are a bad influence for them.

3. A confident person is most likely going to have a positive outlook on life. People filled with positivity have happier lives. This kind of positivity is much needed by teenagers who are frequently faced with meeting new people, being in new situations and even new places. Teenagers need to be confident that despite the changes that they are going through, the can do it. They won't get paralyzed, fearful or even anxious whenever they encounter new situations. Instead, they see it as an opportunity to learn.

So what are the different things that can contribute to a teenager's confidence? There are four main areas that have a huge impact on how confident a teenager is. These areas are:

1. Friends

During the teenage years, friends start to have more influence than the parents. How things go between a teen and their circle of friends can have a huge effect on their confidence level. It is also possible at this stage for kids who have been best of friends since the first year of school to start drifting apart. Teens move from one circle of friends to another until they find the right circle of friends where they feel the most comfortable.

2. Parents

Sometimes it does not feel like it but the relationship that teens have with their parents are still important for them. How intact the relationship stays depends on how willing each party is to listen and how much space a parent can give the teenager. This is a difficult stage because teens want to be treated the way adults are treated however parents still see them as children that are incapable of making decisions on their own.

3. Academic Performance

When a teen does well academically, they are able to get respect from their teacher and parents. But it can also be a conflict because high academic achievers can also be a victim of peer pressure. Teens find it more difficult to concentrate on school when there are many other things that seem to be more fun.

4. Performance in Extracurricular Activities

Teenagers who seem to have trouble maintaining friendships tend to turn to other activities like sports or even music. It is a good way for them to meet new friends and what's even better is that it will be easier to maintain friendships with people in their activity group because they have something in common. A teen who does well in any particular activity will also get compliments and praises from adults like parents and teachers as well as their peers.

Because teenagers go through so many changes in this time of their life, it is easy for them to feel that they are inadequate. It is probably in this time of their life that they will realize that they may not do well in many things. When their confidence starts to dwindle, what can a parent like you do? You will find some tips in the next sections. Make sure that you pay attention to boosting your teen's confidence so that they can continue performing well in school and in everything else.

History Of Teens

Weird as it may seem but did you know that teenage years was not considered as a phase of life that we all go through until the post-Depression era? This does not mean though that people prior to the recognition of teenage years as a life stage did not go through the physical and mental changes that all teenagers go through. However, it was only in the 1940s that teenagers were defined and recognized the way we recognize them now. This is the phase in life where people at this stage have their own fashion, beliefs, issues, language and really weird rituals. So, the term teenager is still relatively new.

Section 1: Boosting A Teen's Confidence

As a teenager goes through different changes, it is common to see some lose the confidence they used to have. Lack of confidence is greater at the beginning of the adolescent years but their confidence level will eventually increase as they start to adapt to the changes that they have gone through. However, not having enough self-confidence is going to be a problem regardless of how old or in which stage of a transition period one is in.

When a teenager does not have enough confidence, they might feel lonely and awkward. They might not respond well to criticisms as well as their shortcomings. Because they don't feel confident, they are likely to isolate themselves and minimize the activities that they involve themselves in. Or if they do have friends, it is easier for a teen that lacks self-confidence to become a victim of bad peer pressure. A lot of things can happen when a teen lacks self-confidence. They could start falling behind in class or start being rebellious or act out in some other ways to get attention. In worst case scenarios, teenager's who do not have enough self-confidence might even resort to drug abuse, smoking and drinking.

So what are the different things that you can do to boost your teen's confidence?

1. Give them chances and opportunities to learn something new and accomplish something. The best way for a teen to get a confidence boost is to place them in situations where they are not quite sure about what they should do yet they need to figure it out.

How do you do this? Enroll them in activities or classes where they can learn something new. It can be an art class, a soccer club, ballet or even singing classes. But you need to remember that the activity that you enroll them to should be something that they like otherwise your teen will only resist your efforts. It does not matter if you are dealing with a toddler or a teenager but as long as you enforce upon your child something that they doe not like then you are likely to encounter resistance and you will only end up with a frustrated child. New activities that they are not quite good at yet are good for your teens but you need to balance this with the other activities where they are already excelling.

Another way that you can help them build their confidence is to give them household chores that you know they are capable of doing like cleaning their room and collecting the laundry. It is also a good way to teach them about responsibility.

2. A teenager will be able to learn to trust themself when you give they unconditional love. This love that you give to your child helps them feel safe. However, you cannot bail your teen out every time they come across a different situation. You may be keeping them safe but you are not allowing them to resolve things on their own and you are not allowing them to trust in themself that they will be able to resolve the problem. What you can do instead when they encounter difficult situations is to let them feel that you love them. Listen to them when they needs you to listen and give them advice when they asks for it. But never do the actual resolution yourself, leave that to your teen.

3. Teenagers will often come across horrific images that are a result of violence. They could be caused by terrorists or just some random guy who decided to go on a random killing spree just because they lost it. These images cannot be avoided especially when your teen spends a considerable amount of time in front of the television or on the internet. But what you can do instead is to talk to your child about this. Let them know that even though these violent acts are happening around the country and around the world, the people living in this world are strong enough and they will be able to pull through and be able to support each other in such times. What are the other things that you can do?

- Make sure that the environment in your home is calm. But if you are feeling anxious, you need to let your children know why you are feeling this way.
- Always assure your teen that the grown-ups are doing all that they can to make sure that it is safe once again.
- Make sure that you listen to what your teen has to say about the issue.
- Do not guess or exaggerate any details. Tell your child the facts instead.
- Prevent your child from too much exposure to violent images.
- You may want to share other historic events that have caused heartaches to people, such as war. It will be a good way for your child to see that even though bad things happen to people that are innocent, it is always possible to get back on our feet and continue with our lives normally. Be very delicate if you bring this up though because it may be too much for your teen to handle if they're already concerned about a modern day incident.

- The normal routine in your home has to continue.

4. Any child, regardless of age, will always appreciate any praise and compliments coming from people that are important to them. When you praise a child for something good that they did or give them a compliment on their project, you are certainly boosting their confidence level. But there is one thing that you need to remember. Your child cannot be deceived as easily when they was younger. They are now in their teenage years and they can easily determine if the compliment or praise that you have given them is real or not. So when you do give out compliments and praises, make sure that you mean them. They need to be genuine.

5. Adults have had their fair share of explorations. We have been able to explore various areas in our lives and we already know which areas we are good at and which areas we are not so good at. Many of us choose to stay and focus on areas that we are very good at. However, teens have not had this chance to determine yet which areas they are good at and which areas they are not. They are just starting their journey. Say for example, your daughter is doing well academically but does not have much experience in dating. However, a lot of her friends are dating already and most of them are telling her that it is fun to be dating and it is important. As an adult, you know that the chance of that boy who just asked her out for a date making a huge impact on her life is slim. Unfortunately, your daughter does not understand this yet. This could make you feel helpless.

Let her make a mistake instead in order for her to realize the things they need to learn on her own. Although you still need to make sure that you supervise her from a distance and you should be there to provide any form of guidance whenever they need it.

6. Children of any age needs boundaries and the same thing still applies for your teenager. You need to set the rules for your teenagers and explain it to them. The boundaries and rules that you set for them should fit well with your lifestyle as a family. So say for example that you are a single mom that has to work during the day, then your teen needs to understand that they need to help around the house before they hang out with friends. Do not just give them orders but instead explain to them why you need them to help around the house. Knowing why they are expected to follow rules will make it easier for them to follow the rules that you have put in place. And when boundaries are set, they need to be followed. There should be no ifs and neither should there be buts.

7. Encourage your child to help in making decisions that involve the whole family. Ask them for their opinion. So are you and your partner planning to take the kids on a vacation? Or are you planning to do some renovations in the house? Whatever it is, take the time to stop and ask your child what they think about an idea or if they have other suggestions. Teenagers like it when they are treated like adults and you are boosting their confidence when you are asking them to be involved in matters like these. However, you should not just be asking for the sake of asking. You need to listen to what they have to say and consider their opinion. You might even be in for a shock when you hear the ideas that your teen has and you might even ask yourself why you never thought of that.

8. Yes, your teenager feels like they will be able to handle anything and everything that life has to throw at them. But come on, your teenager is still going to need you at some point. So you need to make sure that the communication lines between you and your teen are always available. Luckily, in our current generation, there are many ways that we can communicate and distance is no longer an excuse not to communicate. There are video calls, regular phone calls, text messaging, emails, chats, face-to-face talking, the good old snail mail, journals and so on. It is up to you to be creative about this. What's important is that your teen understands that if they need to talk to you about anything, there is no need to hesitate. And when you ask them questions, make sure that they can be answered with more than a yes or a no.

9. You need to respect your teen. They are no longer children now and they are almost adults. You need to respect their private space and the same can be expected from them. It is important that their problems or issues are considered as important and when you talk to them, you need to be respectful.

10. Criticisms are capable of bursting your child's confidence. You need to make sure that you avoid criticisms as much as you can. What you should do instead when you see something that you do not like or approve of is to ask her to sit down so that both of you can talk about it. Point out to her what is wrong or what you dislike, why it is wrong and come up with things that can turn the situation around. But when the time comes that criticisms are inevitable, you need to make sure that you watch the tone of your voice. Teenagers tend to feel ashamed or can even get rebellious when they get criticized.

11. Teasing and even heckling is part of the daily life of a teenager. It's one of the things that they do to have fun. However, some teens are too uptight and easily get offended by such. You need to teach your kid not to get angry or upset when they are teased about something and that they should learn to develop some level of tolerance in order to deal with this. However, like everything else, you also need to teach your teen the boundaries when it comes to the teasing that they should tolerate.

Section 2: Ways To Help Your Teen Excel In School

When you are preparing your teen to get ready for school, it is like preparing a boxer for an upcoming fight. The only difference between your teen and a boxer is your teen's bout happens five times a week for the whole nine months of a school year. With that said, preparing your teen for school is not an easy task. So what are the things that you can do to make sure that your teen is well prepared for school so that they have every chance to excel? Follow the strategies that we have listed below!

1. Many parents think that adolescents that are older need much less sleep than younger adolescents. This is not actually true. Even a ten-hour slumber might not be enough to stop your older teen from falling asleep in the first hour or two of class. This is because the brains of older teens secrete melatonin which is a hormone that induces sleep an hour later than when they were younger. This means that the onset of their sleep is delayed by an hour and they end up missing the most peaceful part of a sleep, the REM sleep.

So what can you do to help out with this? Get your teen to prepare their things for school before going to sleep on a school night so that they can extend their sleep in the morning without having to rush off to school.

2. Many teenagers believe that people are either born smart or not. This is what they usually have in mind as they go through the different changes that they endure during the transition phase. They do not see that how much effort they put into studying is what defines their success or failure. Instead, they consider it to be predestined.

Even when they have low self-confidence, it is still easier for a teenager to deal with the difficult subjects as long as they know the importance of good study habits. These teens will be willing to tackle topics even though they are difficult.

As a parent, it is important that you continue helping your teen develop good study habits. You need to remind them that diligence can go a long way in school. One does not need to be born smart in order to get good grades in an exam.

3. Having an environment that is conducive for learning will go a long way in making sure that your kid is studying when they need to be studying. You can help create this kind of environment in a couple of ways. First of all, your child needs to have a space that they can permanently use as their 'mini-office' where they can do their homework and study as well. Any reference books that they might need like a dictionary should be kept nearby too. The room that you have set as their mini office should also be well-lit and free of things that could distract them from their homework. Turn the television of during the hour or two that your teen will be studying. Even though the TV might be in another room, the sound that your teen hears from the set could still decrease their retention ability. If somebody in the household wants to watch a program that falls during the time when the set is scheduled to be turned off, you can always record it so that it can be watched at a later time. There are some teens though that claim that they are able to concentrate just as much when music is playing in the background. One way for you to judge if you should allow your child to keep the music playing while they are doing is homework or studying is by looking at the results. If the child needs to use a computer, it might be a better idea to keep the computer in a common place where it will be easier for you to monitor what they are doing on the computer.

4. You need to make sure that your teen spends enough time doing their homework or studying. Teens often have so many things to do after classes are over. Some are involved in various extracurricular activities while some take on part-time jobs. So the most common time for teens to do their homework is after dinner. This should not be a problem though because teens can stay up doing homework without falling asleep. However, if you do notice that your teen does not seem to have enough time to do their homework after dinner, you might need to ask them to slow down a little on the extracurricular activities or render an hour or two less at work so that they have enough time to do their homework and to study. Try to talk to their teacher too and see if you can get them to include study hall in their schedule so that they have time to do their homework while in school. For a child to excel in school, it is important that they spend enough time doing their homework and studying too so that they do not fall behind.

5. There will be times when your teen might not be able to understand certain topics, homework/project instructions or is simply having a hard time answering the assignment they have. Make yourself available whenever they have any questions that they need help in. When they ask questions, do not immediately think that they are being lazy. It is actually a good way for them to learn. You also need to remember that being in high school is quite difficult because of the many subjects that they need to master like reading, math, science, language and so on. Have a little patience when they ask you questions. But of course, you need to remember that answering or helping them out does not mean that you should be the one to do their homework. That is not going to help them learn at all. You are teaching your teen instead to be dependent on you to provide the answers for them. You can give them hints about the answer or where to look for the answer but do not answer the homework yourself.

6. You need to determine too if your child is doing too much homework. A teen that is procrastinating and extending their one-hour homework into three hours is not the same as a teen who spends countless hours every night doing their homework. If you notice that your child is doing this, they might be handling way too much workload. If so, you might need to have a discussion with their teacher about this. There is a rule of thumb when it comes to how much homework your child should be doing. According to research, the time spent studying/doing homework should be ten minutes for every grade level. So your sixth grader should only do an hour of homework period everyday while a ninth grader should spend an hour and a half on homework. A child who goes beyond that is not going to make any significant changes in their score exams.

7. Many teenagers today have part-time jobs. This is a good thing because it is a good way for them to learn more about responsibility and managing their finances. It is a great way to build their character too. However, when teens spend too much time working, they may start neglecting their other responsibilities like school. They could end up getting stressed out as they try to balance school, work, extracurricular activities and family time. They might start misbehaving and even start abusing alcohol and even drugs.

Their academic performance can also be affected. They might feel too exhausted and end up falling asleep in class or not being able to focus well on class discussions. They might even start missing out on school and extracurricular activities too.

Because of the possible effects of working long hours while studying, it is recommended that parents like you should set a limit on how many hours your teen works. The maximum number of hours rendered in part-time jobs should be limited to twenty hours per week. Anything more than that can prove to be disastrous for your child.

8. It is also important that you be involved in your teen's school. Many parents assume that once a child is done with middle school, their child no longer needs them to be involved with their school activities. But you need to understand that even though your child is now in high school, you should still attend parent-teacher conferences. This is a good way for you to pick up on any issues that your child is having and to monitor how they are doing in school as well. It is also a good way for you to determine in which area your child needs help in and the best method to help them out. If you can, you could even contact each instructor of your teen just to check up on how they are doing in general. You do not need to wait to see signs of problems to do this.

It would also be a good idea to be involved in one of the parent groups in the school. It's a great way to familiarize yourself with the teaching staff of the school and to keep yourself updated on the events that a school has. If you happen to be a familiar face to the teachers, it might also be easier to get more information on your teen.

9. No matter how smart your teen is, it is not going to be of much help for them if they keep missing out on school. Your teen should only be skipping school during days when is really sick. And in order for you to keep them in a healthy shape, make sure that they get enough sleep/rest and eats nutritious food. When a teen misses too many school days, they will also need to do a lot of catching up. Sometimes too much catching up can be overwhelming and having to do the catching up by themselves adds more pressure too.

10. You need to convey to your teen that in order for them to be able to succeed, they have to go through failures. Not too many teens are cool with this and it can be difficult to deal with failures during a time when everything seems to be changing. You need to be there to remind your teen that one failure is not going to define how their life will go on. We all go through difficult times and sometimes we end up being defeated in certain areas. However, what matters more is our ability to stand up and try again. When we were just toddlers, we did not learn how to walk right away without falling. The more times we fell, the more we learned how to balance ourselves until we are finally able to take the first unassisted steps in our lives. This very same concept of failing and trying again until we succeed is very much applicable to our daily lives too. In order to reach whatever goal we have in mind, we inevitably make mistakes which could result into a learning experience. Every successful person has gone through a set of failures.

11. In the world we live in today, it is rare when we go through a day without using some kind of gadget. We send text messages to people to let them know where we are, how we are doing and other things, random or important. Smart phones, tablets and laptops are great for doing researches on the internet and staying connected with our friends on the social networks. They are great sources of entertainment as well. As useful as they are, the technology and gadgets that we have today can be a great source of distraction as well. Instead of spending a full hour on studying, we take little breaks that lead into long ones so that we can check the latest news on our friends, celebrities, world events and so on, which means school work ends up unfinished.

To help with this, parents need to set a time limit on the use of gadgets. Everyone should put away their gadgets during meal times so that you and your kids will have the time to catch up on today's activities and talk about other things. You and your kids could also set a time when gadgets should be set aside to be able to do homework and to get some sleep. When setting the time limits, make sure that you and your teen discuss this. Do not just impose the rule on him. They need to understand why such a rule has to be put in place. A person who understands the reason behind seemingly ridiculous rules will find it easier to obey the rules. And as a parent, you should also take the lead. You cannot expect your kid to follow the no-gadget rule if you cannot abide to it yourself.

Conclusion

Teenage years can be difficult especially for people who lack self-confidence. When your teen does not have the right level of self-confidence, they might find it difficult to deal with the many issues and changes linked to the teenage years. This is the time when teens are expected to follow specific norms and when they don't fit in, they could end up being bullied. A teen needs to be confident to know that they doe not need to fit in the norms set by their peers just to fit in. Even when your teen has the right abilities to excel in school, they might be afraid to accomplish achievements because their classmates might make fun of them.

There are many ways that you can help your teen boost their confidence. A confident teen not only has a happier life but they also have a better academic performance. they won't fear what others say about their achievements. Neither will they be afraid to speak up. As a parent, you have a very important role to help your child boost their confidence and do better in school as well. The tips that have been provided in the earlier sections can be a great way to help your teen do better.

The most important thing is that you, the parent, will be there to help them every step of the way. It includes being there for them whenever they need your help and being involved in their school activities. It is okay to give your teen some freedom but there has to be limitations. Treat your teen the way you would treat other adults and make them feel that you appreciate them no matter what. Building your teenagers confidence won't happen overnight but by following these tips and having a deeper understanding of what your teen is going through, they will be on the path to improved confidence in no time.

EXPERIENCE
EVERYTHING
PUBLISHING

www.ingramcontent.com/pod-product-compliance
Lightning Source LLC
Chambersburg PA
CBHW071812020426
42331CB00008B/2463